I0163077

Heracles by Euripides

Translated from the Greek by E. P. Coleridge

Euripides is rightly lauded as one of the great dramatists of all time. In his lifetime, he wrote over 90 plays and although only 18 have survived they reveal the scope and reach of his genius.

Euripides is identified with many theatrical innovations that have influenced drama all the way down to modern times, especially in the representation of traditional, mythical heroes as ordinary people in extraordinary circumstances.

As would be expected from a life lived 2,500 years ago, details of it are few and far between. Accounts of his life, written down the ages, do exist but whether much is reliable or surmised is open to debate.

Most accounts agree that he was born on Salamis Island around 480 BC, to mother Cleito and father Mnesarchus, a retailer who lived in a village near Athens. Upon the receipt of an oracle saying that his son was fated to win "crowns of victory", Mnesarchus insisted that the boy should train for a career in athletics.

However, what is clear is that athletics was not to be the way to win crowns of victory. Euripides had been lucky enough to have been born in the era as the other two masters of Greek Tragedy; Sophocles and Æschylus. It was in their footsteps that he was destined to follow.

His first play was performed some thirteen years after the first of Socrates plays and a mere three years after Æschylus had written his classic The Oristria.

Theatre was becoming a very important part of the Greek culture. The Dionysia, held annually, was the most important festival of theatre and second only to the fore-runner of the Olympic games, the Panathenia, held every four years, in appeal.

Euripides first competed in the City Dionysia, in 455 BC, one year after the death of Æschylus, and, incredibly, it was not until 441 BC that he won first prize. His final competition in Athens was in 408 BC. The Bacchae and Iphigenia in Aulis were performed after his death in 405 BC and first prize was awarded posthumously. Altogether his plays won first prize only five times.

Euripides was also a great lyric poet. In Medea, for example, he composed for his city, Athens, "the noblest of her songs of praise". His lyric skills however are not just confined to individual poems: "A play of Euripides is a musical whole....one song echoes motifs from the preceding song, while introducing new ones."

Much of his life and his whole career coincided with the struggle between Athens and Sparta for hegemony in Greece but he didn't live to see the final defeat of his city.

Euripides fell out of favour with his fellow Athenian citizens and retired to the court of Archelaus, king of Macedon, who treated him with consideration and affection.

At his death, in around 406BC, he was mourned by the king, who, refusing the request of the Athenians that his remains be carried back to the Greek city, buried him with much splendor within his own dominions. His tomb was placed at the confluence of two streams, near Arethusa in Macedonia, and a cenotaph was built to his memory on the road from Athens towards the Piraeus.

Index of Contents

THE PERSONS

AMPHITRYON, husband of Alcmena, the mother of HERACLES
MEGARA, wife of HERACLES, daughter of Creon
LYCUS, unlawful King of Thebes
IRIS
MADNESS
MESSENGER
HERACLES, son of Zeus and Alcmena
THESEUS, King of Athens
CHORUS OF OLD MEN OF THEBES

SCENE

Before the palace of Heracles at Thebes.

HERACLES

Nearby stands the altar of Zeus, on the steps of which are now seated **AMPHITRYON**, **MEGARA** and her **SONS** by **HERACLES**. They are seeking refuge at the altar.

AMPHITRYON
What mortal hath not heard of him who shared a wife with Zeus, Amphitryon of Argos, whom on a day Alcaeus, son of Perseus begat, Amphitryon the father of Heracles? He it was dwelt here in Thebes, where from the sowing of the dragon's teeth grew up a crop of earth-born giants; for of these Ares saved a scanty band, and their children's children people the city of Cadmus. Hence sprung Creon, son of Menoeceus, king of this land; and Creon became the father of this lady Megara, whom once all Cadmus' race escorted with the glad music of lutes at her wedding, in the day that Heracles, illustrious chief, led her to my halls. Now he, my son, left Thebes where I was settled, left his wife Megara and her kin, eager to make his home in Argolis, in that walled town which the Cyclopes built, whence I am exiled for the slaying of Electryon; so he, wishing to lighten my affliction and to find a home in his own land, did offer

Eurystheus a mighty price for my recall, even to free the world of savage monsters, whether it was that Hera goaded him to submit to this, or that fate was leagued against him. Divers are the toils he hath accomplished, and last of all hath he passed through the mouth of Taenarus into the halls of Hades to drag to the light that hound with bodies three, and thence is he never returned. Now there is an ancient legend amongst the race of Cadmus, that one Lycus in days gone by was husband to Dirce being king of this city with its seven towers, before that Amphion and Zethus, sons of Zeus, lords of the milk-white steeds, became rulers in the land. His son, called by the same name as his father, albeit no Theban but a stranger from Euboea, slew Creon, and after that seized the government, having fallen on this city when weakened by dissension. So this connection with Creon is likely to prove to us a serious evil; for now that my son is in the bowels of the earth, this illustrious monarch Lycus is bent on extirpating the children of Heracles, to quench one bloody feud with another, likewise his wife and me, if useless age like mine is to rank amongst men, that the boys may never grow up to exact a blood-penalty of their uncle's family. So I, left here by my son, whilst he is gone into the pitchy darkness of the earth, to tend and guard his children in his house, am taking my place with their mother, that the race of Heracles may not perish, here at the altar of Zeus the Saviour, which my own gallant child set up to commemorate his glorious victory over the Minyae. And here we are careful to keep our station, though in need of everything, of food, of drink, and raiment, huddled together on the hard bare ground; for we are barred out from our house and sit here for want of any other safety. As for friends, some I see are insincere; while others, who are staunch, have no power to help us further. This is what misfortune means to man; God grant it may never fall to the lot of any who bears the least goodwill to me, to apply this never-failing test of friendship!

MEGARA

Old warrior, who erst did raze the citadel of the Taphians leading on the troops of Thebes to glory, how uncertain are God's dealings with man! For I, as far as concerned my sire was never an outcast of fortune, for he was once accounted a man of might by reason of his wealth, possessed as he was of royal power, for which long spears are launched at the lives of the fortunate through love of it; children too he had; and me did he betroth to thy son, matching me in glorious marriage with Heracles. Whereas now all that is dead and gone from us; and I and thou, old friend, art doomed to die, and these children of Heracles, whom I am guarding 'neath my wing as a bird keepeth her tender chicks under her. And they the while in turn keep asking me, "Mother, whither is our father gone from the land? what is he about? when will he return?" Thus they inquire for their father, in childish perplexity; while I put them off with excuses, inventing stories; but still I wonder if 'tis he whenever a door creaks on its hinges, and up they all start, thinking to embrace their father's knees. What hope or way of salvation art thou now devising, old friend? for to thee I look. We can never steal beyond the boundaries of the land unseen, for there is too strict a watch set on us at every outlet, nor have we any longer hopes of safety in our friends. Whatever thy scheme is, declare it, lest our death be made ready, while we are only prolonging the time, powerless to escape.

AMPHITRYON

'Tis by no means easy, my daughter, to give one's earnest advice on such matters easily, without weary thought.

MEGARA

Dost need a further taste of grief, or cling so fast to life?

AMPHITRYON

Yes, I love this life, and cling to its hopes.

MEGARA
So do I; but it boots not to expect the unexpected, old friend.

AMPHITRYON
In these delays is left the only cure for our evils.

MEGARA
'Tis the pain of that interval I feel so.

AMPHITRYON
Daughter, there may yet be a happy escape from present troubles for me and thee; my son, thy husband, may yet arrive. So calm thyself, and wipe those tears from thy children's eyes, and soothe them with soft words, inventing a tale to delude them, piteous though such fraud be. Yea, for men's misfortunes ofttimes flag, and the stormy wind doth not always blow so strong, nor are the prosperous ever so; for all things change, making way for each other. The bravest man is he who relieth ever on his hopes, but despair is the mark of a coward.

[The **CHORUS OF OLD MEN OF THEBES** enters.]

CHORUS [chanting, strophe]
To the sheltering roof, to the old man's couch, leaning on my staff have I set forth, chanting a plaintive dirge like some bird grown grey, I that am but a voice and nothing more, a fancy bred of the visions of sleep by night, palsied with age, yet meaning kindly. All hail! ye orphaned babes! all hail, old friend thou too, -unhappy mother, wailing for thy husband in the halls of Hades!

[antistrophe]
Faint not too soon upon your way, nor let your limbs grow weary, even as a colt beneath the yoke grows weary as he mounts some stony hill, dragging the weight of a wheeled car. Take hold of hand or robe, whoso feels his footsteps falter. Old friend, escort another like thyself, who erst amid his toiling peers in the days of our youth would take his place beside thee, no blot upon his country's glorious record.

See, how like their father's sternly flash these children's eyes! Misfortune, God wot, hath not failed his children, nor yet hath his comeliness been denied them. O Hellas! if thou lose these, of what allies wilt thou rob thyself!

LEADER OF THE CHORUS
But I see Lycus, the ruler of this land, drawing near the house.

[**LYCUS** and his **ATTENDANTS** enter.]

LYCUS
One question, if I may, to this father of Heracles and his wife; and certainly as your lord and master I have a right to put what questions choose. How long do ye seek to prolong your lives? What hope, what succour do ye see to save you from death? Do you trust that these children's father, who lies dead in the halls of Hades, will return? How unworthily ye show your sorrow at having to die, thou [To **AMPHITRYON**] after thy idle boasts, scattered broadcast through Hellas, that Zeus was partner in thy

marriage-bed and there begat a new god; and thou [To **MEGARA**] after calling thyself the wife of so peerless a lord.

After all, what was the fine exploit thy husband achieved, if he did kil a hydra in a marsh or that monster of Nemea? which he caught in a snare, for all he says he strangled it to death in his arms. Are these your weapons for the hard struggle? Is it for this then that Heracles' children should be spared? a man who has won a reputation for valour in his contests with beasts, in all else a weakling; who ne'er buckled shield to arm nor faced the spear, but with a bow, that coward's weapon, was ever ready to run away. Archery is no test of manly bravery; no! he is a man who keeps his post in the ranks and steadily faces the swift wound the spear may plough. My policy, again, old man, shows no reckless cruelty, but caution; for I am well aware I slew Creon, the father of Megara, and am in possession of his throne. So I have no wish that these children should grow up and be left to take vengeance on me in requital for what I have done.

AMPHITRYON
As for Zeus, let Zeus defend his son's case; but as for me, Heracles, I am only anxious on thy behalf to prove by what I say this tyrant's ignorance; for I cannot allow thee to be ill spoken of. First then for that which should never have been said,-for to speak of thee Heracles as coward is, methinks, outside the pale of speech,-of that must I clear the with heaven to witness. I appeal then to the thunder of Zeus, and the chariot wherein he rode, when he pierced the giants, earth's brood, to the heart with his winged shafts, and with gods uplifted the glorious triumph-song; or go to Pholoe and ask the insolent tribe of four-legged Centaurs, thou craven king, ask them who they would judge their bravest foe; will they not say my son, who according to thee is but a pretender? Wert thou to ask Euboean Dirphys, thy native place, it would nowise sing thy praise, for thou hast never done a single gallant deed to which thy country can witness. Next thou dost disparage that clever invention, an archer's weapon; come, listen to me and learn wisdom. A man who fights in line is a slave to his weapons, and if his fellow-comrades want for courage he is slain himself through the cowardice of his neighbours, or, if he break his spear, he has not wherewithal to defend his body from death, having only one means of defence; whereas all who are armed with the trusty bow, though they have but one weapon, yet is it the best; for a man, after discharging countless arrows, still has others wherewith to defend himself from death, and standing at a distance keeps off the enemy, wounding them for all their watchfulness with shafts invisible, and never exposing himself to the foe, but keeping under cover; and this is far the wisest course in battle, to harm the enemy, if they are not stationed out of shot, and keep safe oneself. These arguments are completely opposite to thine with regard to the point at issue. Next, why art thou desirous of slaying these children? What have they done to thee? One piece of wisdom credit thee with, thy coward terror of a brave man's descendants. Still it is hard on us, if for thy cowardice we must die; a fate that ought to have overtaken thee at our braver hands, if Zeus had been fairly disposed towards us. But, if thou art so anxious to make thyself supreme in the land, let us at least go into exile; abstain from all violence, else thou wilt suffer by it whenso the deity causes fortune's breeze to veer round.

Ah! thou land of Cadmus,-for to thee too will I turn, upbraiding thee with words of reproach,-is this your succour of Heracles and his children? the man who faced alone the Minyan host in battle and allowed Thebes to see the light with freemen's eyes. I cannot praise Hellas, nor will I ever keep silence, finding her so craven as regards my son; she should have come with fire and sword and warrior's arms to help these tender babes, to requite him for all his labours in purging land and sea. Such help, my children, neither Hellas nor the city of Thebes affords you; to me a feeble friend ye look, that am but empty sound and nothing more. For the vigour which once I had, is gone from me; my limbs are palsied with age, and my strength is decayed. Were I but young and still a man of my hands, I would have seized my spear and dabbled those flaxen locks of his with blood, so that the coward would now be flying from my prowess beyond the bounds of Atlas.

LEADER OF THE CHORUS
Have not the brave amongst mankind a fair opening for speech, albeit slow to begin?

LYCUS
Say what thou wilt of me in thy exalted phrase, but I by deeds will make thee rue those words. [Calling to his **SERVANTS**] Ho! bid wood-cutters go, some to Helicon, others to the glens of Parnassus, and cut me logs of oak, and when they are brought to the town, pile up a stack of wood all round the altar on either side thereof, and set fire to it and burn them all alive, that they may learn that the dead no longer rules this land, but that for the present I am king. [angrily to the **CHORUS**] As for you, old men, since ye thwart my views, not for the children of Heracles alone shall ye lament but likewise for every blow that strikes his house, and ye shall ne'er forget ye are slaves and I your prince.

LEADER
Ye sons of Earth, whom Ares on a day did sow, when from the dragon's ravening jaw he had torn the teeth, up with your staves, whereon ye lean your hands, and dash out this miscreant's brains! a fellow who, without even being a Theban, but a foreigner, lords it shamefully o'er the younger folk; but my master shalt thou never be to thy joy, nor shalt thou reap the harvest of all my toil; begone with my curse upon thee! carry thy insolence back to the place whence it came. For never whilst I live, shalt thou slay these sons of Heracles; not so deep beneath the earth hath their father disappeared from his children's ken. Thou art in possession of this land which thou hast ruined, while he its benefactor has missed his just reward; and yet do I take too much upon myself because I help those I love after their death, when most they need a friend? Ah! right hand, how fain wouldst thou wield the spear, but thy weakness is a death-blow to thy fond desire; for then had I stopped thee calling me slave, and I would have governed Thebes, wherein thou art now exulting, with credit; for city sick with dissension and evil counsels thinketh not aright; otherwise it would never have accepted thee as its master.

MEGARA
Old sirs, I thank you; 'tis right that friends should feel virtuous indignation on behalf of those they love; but do not on our account vent your anger on the tyrant to your own undoing. Hear my advice, Amphitryon, if haply there appear to thee to be aught in what I say. I love my children; strange if I did not love those whom I laboured to bring forth! Death I count a dreadful fate; but the man who wrestles with necessity I esteem a fool. Since we must die, let us do so without being burnt alive, to furnish our foes with food for merriment, which to my mind is an evil worse than death; for many a fair guerdon do we owe our family. Thine has ever been a warrior's fair fame, so 'tis not to be endured that thou shouldst die a coward's death; and my husband's reputation needs no one to witness that he would ne'er consent to save these children's lives by letting them incur the stain of cowardice; for the noble are afflicted by disgrace on account of their children, nor must I shrink from following my lord's example. As to thy hopes consider how I weigh them. Thou thinkest thy son will return from beneath the earth: who ever has come back from the dead out of the halls of Hades? Thou hast a hope perhaps of softening this man by entreaty: no, no! better to fly from one's enemy when he is so brutish, but yield to men of breeding and wisdom; for thou wilt more easily obtain mercy there by friendly overtures. True, a thought has already occurred to me that we might by entreaty obtain a sentence of exile for the children; yet this too is misery, to compass their deliverance with dire penury as the result; for 'tis a saying that hosts look sweetly on banished friends for a day and no more. Steel thy heart to die with us, for that awaits thee after all. By thy brave soul I challenge thee, old friend; for whoso struggles hard to

escape destiny shows zeal no doubt, but 'tis zeal with a taint of folly; for what must be, no one will ever avail to alter.

LEADER
If a man had insulted thee, while yet my arms were lusty, there would have been an easy way to stop him; but now am I a thing of naught; and so thou henceforth, Amphitryon, must scheme how to avert misfortune.

AMPHITRYON
'Tis not cowardice or any longing for life that hinders my dying, but my wish to save my son's children, though no doubt I am vainly wishing for impossibilities. Lo! here is my neck ready for thy sword to pierce, my body for thee to hack or hurl from the rock; only one boon I crave for both of us, O king; slay me and this hapless mother before thou slay the children, that we may not see the hideous sight, as they gasp out their lives, calling on their mother and their father's sire; for the rest work thy will, if so thou art inclined; for we have no defence against death.

MEGARA
I too implore thee add a second boon, that by thy single act thou mayst put us both under a double obligation; suffer me to deck my children in the robes of death,-first opening the palace gates, for now are we shut out,-that this at least they may obtain from their father's halls.

LYCUS
I grant it, and bid my servants undo the bolts. Go in and deck yourselves; robes I grudge not. But soon as ye have clothed yourselves, I will return to you to consign you to the nether world.

[**LYCUS** and his **RETINUE** withdraw.]

MEGARA
Children, follow the footsteps of your hapless mother to your father's halls, where others possess his substance, though his name is still ours.

[**MEGARA** and her **CHILDREN** enter the palace.]

AMPHITRYON
O Zeus, in vain it seems, did I get thee to share my bride with me; in vain used we to call thee father of my son. After all thou art less our friend than thou didst pretend. Great god as thou art, I, a mere mortal, surpass thee in true worth. For I did not betray the children of Heracles; but thou by stealth didst find thy way to my couch, taking another's wife without leave given, while to save thy own friends thou hast no skill. Either thou art a god of little sense, or else naturally unjust.

[**AMPHITRYON** follows **MEGARA** into the palace.]

CHORUS [singing, strophe 1]
Phoebus is singing a plaintive dirge to drown his happier strains, striking with key of gold his sweet-tongued lyre; so too am I fain to sing a song of praise, a crown to all his toil, concerning him who is gone to the gloom beneath the nether world, whether I am to call him son of Zeus or of Amphitryon. For the praise of noble toils accomplished is a glory to the dead. First he cleared the grove of Zeus of a lion, and put its skin upon his back, hiding his auburn hair in its fearful gaping jaws;

[antistrophe 1]
Then on a day, with murderous bow he wounded the race of wild Centaurs, that range the hills, slaying them with winged shafts; Peneus, the river of fair eddies, knows him well, and those far fields unharvested, and the steadings on Pelion and they who haunt the glens of Homole bordering thereupon, whence they rode forth to conquer Thessaly, arming themselves with pines for clubs; likewise he slew that dappled hind with horns of gold, that preyed upon the country-folk, glorifying Artemis, huntress queen of Oenoe;

[strophe 2]
Next he mounted on a car and tamed with the bit the steeds of Diomede, that greedily champed their bloody food at gory mangers with jaws unbridled, devouring with hideous joy the flesh of men; then crossing Hebrus' silver stream he still toiled on to perform the hests of the tyrant of Mycenae, till he came to the strand of the Malian gulf by the streams of Anaurus, where he slew with his arrows Cycnus, murderer of his guests, the savage wretch who dwelt in Amphanae;

[antistrophe 2]
Also he came to those minstrel maids, to their orchard in the west, to pluck from the leafy apple-tree its golden fruit, when he had slain the tawny dragon, whose awful coils were twined all round to guard it; and he made his way into ocean's lairs, bringing calm to men that use the oar; moreover he sought the home of Atlas, and stretched out his hands to uphold the firmament, and on his manly shoulders took the starry mansions of the gods;

[strophe 3]
Then he went through the waves of heaving Euxine against the mounted host of Amazons dwelling round Maeotis, the lake that is fed by many a stream, having gathered to his standard all his friends from Hellas, to fetch the gold-embroidered raiment of the warrior queen, a deadly quest for a girdle. And Hellas won those glorious spoils of the barbarian maid, and safe in Mycenae are they now. On Lerna's murderous hound, the many-headed hydra, he set his branding-iron, and smeared its venom on his darts, wherewith he slew the shepherd of Erytheia, a monster with three bodies;

[antistrophe 3]
And many another glorious achievement he brought to a happy issue; to Hades' house of tears hath he now sailed, the goal of his labours, where he is ending his career of toil, nor cometh he thence again. Now is thy house left without a friend, and Charon's boat awaits thy children to bear them on that journey out of life, whence is no returning, contrary to God's law and man's justice; and it is to thy prowess that thy house is looking although thou art not here. Had I been strong and lusty, able to brandish the spear in battle's onset, my Theban compeers too, I would have stood by thy children to champion them; but now my happy youth is gone and I am left.

But lo! I see the children of Heracles who was erst so great, clad in the vesture of the grave, and his loving wife dragging her babes along at her side, and that hero's aged sire. Ah! woe is me! no longer can I stem the flood of tears that spring to my old eyes.

[**MEGARA**, **AMPHITRYON**, and the **CHILDREN** enter from the palace.]

MEGARA

Come now, who is to sacrifice or butcher these poor children? or rob me of my wretched life? Behold! the victims are ready to be led to Hades' halls. O my children! an ill-matched company are we hurried off to die, old men and babes, and mothers, all together. Alas! for my sad fate and my children's, whom these eyes now for the last time behold. So I gave you birth and reared you only for our foes to mock, to flout, and slay. Ah me! how bitterly my hopes have disappointed me in the expectation once formed from the words of your father.

[Addressing each of her **SONS** in turn]

To thee thy dead sire was for giving Argos; and thou wert to dwell in the halls of Eurystheus, lording it o'er the fair fruitful land of Argolis; and o'er thy head would he throw that lion's skin wherewith himself was girt. Thou wert to be king of Thebes, famed for its chariots, receiving as thy heritage my broad lands, for so thou didst coax thy father dear; and to thy hand used he to resign the carved club, his sure defence, pretending to give it thee. To thee he promised to give Oechalia, which once his archery had wasted. Thus with three principalities would your father exalt you his three sons, proud of your manliness; while I was choosing the best brides for you, scheming to link you by marriage to Athens, Thebes, and Sparta, that ye might live a happy life with a fast sheet-anchor to hold by. And now that is all vanished; fortune's breeze hath veered and given to you for brides the maidens of death in their stead, and tears to me to bathe them in; woe is me for my foolish thoughts and your grandsire here is celebrating your marriage-feast, accepting Hades as the father of your brides, a grim relationship to make. Ah me! which of you shall I first press to my bosom, which last? on which bestow my kiss, or clasp close to me? Oh! would that like the bee with russet wing, I could collect from every source my sighs in one, and, blending them together, shed them in one copious flood! Heracles, dear husband mine, to thee I call, if haply mortal voice can make itself heard in Hades' halls; thy father and children are dying and I am doomed, I who once because of thee was counted blest as men count bliss. Come to our rescue; appear, I pray, if but as a phantom, since thy mere coming would be enough, for they are cowards compared with thee, who are slaying thy children.

AMPHITRYON
Lady, do thou prepare the funeral rites; but I, O Zeus, stretching out my hand to heaven, call on thee to help these children, if such be thy intention; for soon will any aid of thine be unavailing; and yet thou hast been oft invoked; my toil is wasted; death seems inevitable. Ye aged friends, the joys of life are few; so take heed that ye pass through it as gladly as ye may, without a thought of sorrow from morn till night; for time recks little of preserving our hopes; and, when he has busied himself on his own business, away he flies. Look at me, a man who had made mark amongst his fellows by deeds of note; yet hath fortune in a single day robbed me of it as of a feather that floats away toward the sky. know not any whose plenteous wealth and high reputation is fixed and sure; fare ye well, for now have ye seen the last of your old friend, my comrades.

[**MEGARA** catches sight of **HERACLES** approaching.]

MEGARA
Ha! old friend, is it my own, my dearest I behold? or what am I to say?

AMPHITRYON
I know not, my daughter; I too am struck dumb.

MEGARA

Is this he who, they told us, was beneath the earth?

AMPHITRYON
'Tis he, unless some day-dream mocks our sight.

MEGARA
What am I saying? What visions do these anxious eyes behold? Old man, this is none other than thy own son. Come hither, my children, cling to your father's robe, make haste to come, never loose your hold, for here is one to help you, nowise behind our saviour Zeus.

[**HERACLES** enters.]

HERACLES
All hail! my house, and portals of my home, how glad am I to emerge to the light and see thee. Ha! what is this? I see my children before the house in the garb of death, with chaplets on their heads, my wife amid a throng of men, and my father weeping o'er some mischance. Let me draw near to them and inquire; lady, what strange stroke of fate hath fallen on the house?

MEGARA
Dearest of all mankind to me! O ray of light appearing to thy sire! art thou safe, and is thy coming just in time to help thy dear ones?

HERACLES
What meanest thou? what is this confusion I find on my arrival, father?

MEGARA
We are being ruined; forgive me, old friend, if I have anticipated that which thou hadst a right to tell him; for woman's nature is perhaps more prone than man's to grief, and they are my children that were being led to death, which was my own lot too.

HERACLES
Great Apollo! what a prelude to thy story!

MEGARA
Dead are my brethren, dead my hoary sire.

HERACLES
How so? what befell him? who dealt the fatal blow?

MEGARA
Lycus, our splendid monarch, slew him.

HERACLES
Did he meet him in fair fight, or was the land sick and weak?

MEGARA
Aye, from faction; now is he master of the city of Cadmus with its seven gates.

HERACLES

Why hath panic fallen on thee and my aged sire?

MEGARA

He meant to kill thy father, me, and my children.

HERACLES

Why, what had he to fear from my orphan babes?

MEGARA

He was afraid they might some day avenge Creon's death.

HERACLES

What means this dress they wear, suited to the dead?

MEGARA

'Tis the garb of death we have already put on.

HERACLES

And were ye being haled to death? O woe is me!

MEGARA

Yes, deserted by every friend, and informed that thou wert dead.

HERACLES

What put such desperate thoughts into your heads?

MEGARA

That was what the heralds of Eurystheus kept proclaiming.

HERACLES

Why did ye leave my hearth and home?

MEGARA

He forced us; thy father was dragged from his bed.

HERACLES

Had he no mercy, to ill-use the old man so?

MEGARA

Mercy forsooth! that goddess and he dwell far enough apart.

HERACLES

Was I so poor in friends in my absence?

MEGARA

Who are the friends of a man in misfortune?

HERACLES

Do they make so light of my hard warring with the Minyae?

MEGARA

Misfortune, to repeat it to thee, has no friends.

HERACLES

Cast from your heads these chaplets of death, look up to the light, for instead of the nether gloom your eyes behold the welcome sun. I, meantime, since here is work for my hand, will first go raze this upstart tyrant's halls, and when I have beheaded the miscreant, I will throw him to dogs to tear; and every Theban who I find has played the traitor after my kindness, will I destroy with this victorious club; the rest will I scatter with my feathered shafts and fill Ismenus full of bloody corpses, and Dirce's clear fount shall run red with gore. For whom ought I to help rather than wife and children and aged sire? Farewell my labours! for it was in vain I accomplished them rather than succoured these. And yet I ought to die in their defence, since they for their sire were doomed; else what shall we find so noble in having fought a hydra and a lion at the hests of Eurystheus, if I make no effort to save my own children from death? No longer I trow, as heretofore, shall I be called Heracles the victor.

LEADER OF THE CHORUS

'Tis only right that parents should help their children, their aged sires, and the partners of their marriage.

AMPHITRYON

My son, 'tis like thee to show thy love for thy dear ones and thy hate for all that is hostile; only curb excessive hastiness.

HERACLES

Wherein, father, am I now showing more than fitting haste?

AMPHITRYON

The king hath a host of allies, needy villains though pretending to be rich, who sowed dissension and o'erthrew the state with a view to plundering their neighbours; for the wealth they had in their houses was all spent, dissipated by their sloth. Thou wast seen entering the city; and, that being so, beware that thou bring not thy enemies together and be slain unawares.

HERACLES

Little I reck if the whole city saw me; but chancing to see a bird perched in an ill-omened spot, from it I learnt that some trouble had befallen my house; so I purposely made my entry to the land by stealth.

AMPHITRYON

For thy lucky coming hither, go salute thy household altar, and let thy father's halls behold thy face. For soon will the king be here in person to drag away thy wife and children and murder them, and to add me to the bloody list. But if thou remain on the spot all will go well, and thou wilt profit by this security; but do not rouse thy city ere thou hast these matters well in train, my son.

HERACLES

I will do so; thy advice is good; I will enter my house. After my return at length from the sunless den of Hades and the maiden queen of hell, I will not neglect to greet first of all the gods beneath my roof.

AMPHITRYON

Why, didst thou in very deed go to the house of Hades, my son?

HERACLES

Aye, and brought to the light that three-headed monster.

AMPHITRYON

Didst worst him in fight, or receive him from the goddess?

HERACLES

In fair fight; for I had been lucky enough to witness the rites of the initiated.

AMPHITRYON

Is the monster really lodged in the house of Eurystheus?

HERACLES

The grove of Demeter and the city of Hermione are his prison.

AMPHITRYON

Does not Eurystheus know that thou hast returned to the upper world?

HERACLES

He knows not; I came hither first to learn your news.

AMPHITRYON

How is it thou wert so long beneath the earth?

HERACLES

I stayed awhile attempting to bring back Theseus from Hades, father.

AMPHITRYON

Where is he? gone to his native land?

HERACLES

He set out for Athens right glad to have escaped from the lower world. Come, children, attend your father to the house. My entering in is fairer in your eyes, I trow, than my going out. Take heart, and no more let the tears stream from your eyes; thou too, dear wife, collect thy courage, cease from fear; let go my robe; for I cannot fly away, nor have I any wish to flee from those I love. Ah! they do not loose their hold, but cling to my garments all the more; were ye in such jeopardy? Well, I must lead them, taking them by the hand to draw them after me, like a ship when towing; for I too do not reject the care of my children; here all mankind are equal; all love their children, both those of high estate and those; who are naught; 'tis wealth that makes distinctions among them; some have, others want; but all the human race loves its offspring.

[**HERACLES, MEGARA, AMPHITRYON** and the **CHILDREN** enter the palace.]

CHORUS [singing, strophe 1]

Dear to me is youth, but old age is ever hanging o'er my head, a burden heavier than Aetna's crags, casting its pall of gloom upon my eyes. Oh! never may the wealth of Asia's kings tempt me to barter for houses stored with gold my happy youth, which is in wealth and poverty alike most fair! But old age is gloomy and deathly; I hate it; let it sink beneath the waves! Would it had never found its way to the homes and towns of mortal men, but were still drifting on for ever down the wind.

[antistrophe 1]
Had the gods shown discernment and wisdom, as mortals count these things, men would have gotten youth twice over, a visible mark of worth amongst whomsoever found, and after death would these have retraced their steps once more to the sun-light, while the mean man would have had but a single portion of life; and thus would it have been possible to distinguish the good and the bad, just as sailors know the number of the stars amid the clouds. But, as it is, the gods have set no certain boundary 'twixt good and bad, but time's onward roll brings increase only to man's wealth.

[strophe 2]
Never will I cease to link in one the Graces and the Muses, fairest union. Never may my lines be cast among untutored boors, but ever may I find a place among the crowned choir! Yes, still the aged bard lifts up his voice of bygone memories; still is my song of the triumphs of Heracles, whether Bromius the giver of wine is nigh, or the strains of the seven-stringed lyre and the Libyan flute are rising; not yet will I cease to sing the Muses' praise, my patrons in the dance.

[antistrophe 2]
As the maids of Delos raise their song of joy, circling round the temple gates in honour of Leto's fair son, the graceful dancer; so with my old lips will sing songs of victory at thy palace-doors, song of my old age, such as sings the dying swan; for there is a goodly theme for minstrelsy; he is the son of Zeus; yet high above his noble birth tower his deeds of prowess, for his toil secured this life of calm for man, having destroyed all fearsome beasts.

[**AMPHITRYON** comes out of the palace as **LYCUS** and his **RETINUE** enter.]

LYCUS
Ha! Amphitryon, 'tis high time thou camest forth from the palace; ye have been too long arraying yourselves in the robes and trappings of the dead. Come, bid the wife and children of Heracles show themselves outside the house, to die on the conditions you yourselves offered.

AMPHITRYON
O king, thou dost persecute me in my misery and heapest insult upon me over and above the loss of my son; thou shouldst have been more moderate in thy zeal, though thou art my lord and master. But since thou dost impose death's stern necessity on me, needs must I acquiesce and do thy will.

LYCUS
Pray, where is Megara? where are the children of Alcmena's son?

AMPHITRYON
She, I believe, so far as I can guess from outside-

LYCUS
What grounds hast thou to base thy fancy on?

AMPHITRYON

Is sitting as a suppliant on the altar's hallowed steps.

LYCUS

Imploring them quite uselessly to save her life.

AMPHITRYON

And calling on her dead husband, quite in vain.

LYCUS

He is nowhere near, and he certainly will never come.

AMPHITRYON

No, unless perhaps a god should raise him from the dead.

LYCUS

Go to her and bring her from the palace.

AMPHITRYON

By doing so I should become an accomplice in her murder.

LYCUS

Since thou hast this scruple, I, who have left fear behind, will myself bring out the mother and her children. Follow me, servants, that we may put an end to this delay of our work to our joy.

[**LYCUS** and his **SERVANTS** enter the palace.]

AMPHITRYON

Then go thy way along the path of fate; for what remains, maybe another will provide. Expect for thy evil deeds to find some ill thyself. Ah! my aged friends, he is marching fairly to his doom; soon will he be entangled in the snare of the sword, thinking to slay his neighbours, the villain! I will hence, to see him fall dead; for the sight of a foe being slain and paying the penalty of his misdeeds gives pleasure.

[**AMPHITRYON** follows **LYCUS** into the palace.]

CHORUS [singing]

Evil has changed sides; he who was erst a mighty king is now turning his life backward into the road to Hades.

Hail to thee! justice and heavenly retribution.
At last hast thou reached the goal where thy death will pay the forfeit,

For thy insults against thy betters.
Joy makes my tears burst forth.
There is come a retribution, which the prince of the land never once thought in his heart would happen.

Come, old friends, let us look within to see if one we know has met the fate I hope.

LYCUS [within]
Ah me! ah me!

CHORUS [singing]
Ha! how sweet to hear that opening note of his within the house; death is not far off him now.

Hark! the prince cries out in his agony; that preludes death.

LYCUS [within]
O kingdom of Cadmus, by treachery I am perishing!

CHORUS [singing]
Thou wert thyself for making others perish; endure thy retribution; 'tis only the penalty of thy own deeds thou art paying.

Who was he, weak son of man, that aimed his silly saying at the blessed gods of heaven with impious blasphemy, maintaining that they are weaklings after all?

Old friends, our godless foe is now no more.
The house is still; let us to our dancing.
Yea, for fortune smiles upon my friends as I desire.

[strophe 1]
Dances and banquets now prevail throughout the holy town of Thebes.
For release from tears and respite from sorrow give birth to song.
The upstart king is dead and gone; our former monarch now is prince, having made his way even from the bourn of Acheron. Hope beyond all expectation is fulfilled.

[antistrophe 1]
To heed the right and wrong is heaven's care. 'Tis their gold and their good luck that lead men's hearts astray, bringing in their train unholy tyranny. For no man ever had the courage to reflect what reverses time might bring; but, disregarding law to gratify lawlessness, he shatters in gloom the car of happiness.

[strophe 2]
Deck thee with garlands, O Ismenus! break forth into dancing, ye paved streets of our seven-gated city! come Dirce, fount of waters fair; and joined with her ye daughters of Asopus, come from your father's waves to add your maiden voices to our hymn, the victor's prize that Heracles hath won. O Pythian rock, with forests crowned, and haunts of the Muses on Helicon! make my city and her walls re-echo with cries of joy; where sprang the earth-born crop to view, a warrior-host with shields of brass, who are handing on their realm to children's children, a light divine to Thebes.

[antistrophe 2]
All hail the marriage! wherein two bridegrooms shared; the one, a mortal; the other, Zeus, who came to wed the maiden sprung from Perseus; for that marriage of thine, O Zeus, in days gone by has been proved to me a true story beyond all expectation; and time hath shown the lustre of Heracles' prowess, who emerged from caverns 'neath the earth after leaving Pluto's halls below. To me art thou a worthier

lord than that base-born king, who now lets it be plainly seen in this struggle 'twixt armed warriors, whether justice still finds favour in heaven.

[The spectres of **MADNESS** and **IRIS** appear from above. The **CHORUS** sees them.]

Ha! see there, my old comrades! is the same wild panic fallen on us all; what phantom is this I see hovering o'er the house? Fly, fly, bestir thy tardy steps! begone! away! away! O savior prince, avert calamity from me!

IRIS

Courage, old men! she, whom you see, is Madness, daughter of Night, and I am Iris, the handmaid of the gods. We have not come to do your city any hurt, but against the house of one man only is our warfare, even against him whom they call the son of Zeus and Alcmena. For until he had finished all his grievous toils, Destiny was preserving him, nor would father Zeus ever suffer me or Hera to harm him. But now that he hath accomplished the labours of Eurystheus, Hera is minded to brand him with the guilt of shedding kindred blood by slaying his own children, and I am one with her. Come then, maid unwed, child of murky Night, harden thy heart relentlessly, send forth frenzy upon him, confound his mind even to the slaying of his children, drive him, goad him wildly on his mad career, shake out the sails of death, that when he has sent o'er Acheron's ferry that fair group of children by his own murderous hand, he may learn to know how fiercely against him the wrath of Hera burns and may also experience mine; otherwise, if he escape punishment, the gods will become as naught, while man's power will grow.

MADNESS

Of noble parents was I born, the daughter of Night, sprung from the blood of Uranus; and these prerogatives I hold, not to use them in anger against friends, nor have I any joy in visiting the homes of men; and fain would I counsel Hera, before I see her err, and thee too, if ye will hearken to my words. This man, against whose house thou art sending me, has made himself a name alike in heaven and earth; for, after taming pathless wilds and raging sea, he by his single might raised up again the honours of the gods when sinking before man's impiety; wherefore I counsel thee, do not wish him dire mishaps.

IRIS

Spare us thy advice on Hera's and my schemes.

MADNESS

I seek to turn thy steps into the best path instead of into this one of evil.

IRIS

'Twas not to practice self-control that the wife of Zeus sent thee hither.

MADNESS

I call the sun-god to witness that herein I am acting against my will; but if indeed I must forthwith serve thee and Hera and follow you in full cry as hounds follow the huntsman, why go I will; nor shall ocean with its moaning waves, nor the earthquake, nor the thunderbolt with blast of agony be half so furious as the headlong rush I will make into the breast of Heracles; through his roof will I burst my way and swoop upon his house, after first slaying his children; nor shall their murderer know that he is killing his own-begotten babes, till he is released from my madness. Behold him! see how even now he is wildly tossing his head at the outset, and rolling his eyes fiercely from side to side without word; nor can he control his panting breath; but like a bull in act to charge, he bellows fearfully, calling on the goddesses of nether hell. Soon will I rouse thee to yet wilder dancing and sound a note of terror in thine ear. Soar away, O Iris, to Olympus on thy honoured course; while I unseen will steal into the halls of Heracles.

[IRIS and MADNESS vanish.]

CHORUS [chanting]
Alas! alas! lament, O city; the son of Zeus, thy fairest bloom, is being cut down.

Woe is thee, Hellas! that wilt cast from thee thy benefactor, and destroy him as he madly, wildly dances where no pipe is heard.

She is mounted on her car, the queen of sorrow and sighing, and is goading on her steeds, as if for outrage, the Gorgon child of Night, with hundred hissing serpent-heads, Madness of the flashing eyes.

Soon hath the god changed his good fortune; soon will his children breathe their last, slain by a father's hand.

Ah me! alas! soon will vengeance, mad, relentless, lay low by cruel death thy unhappy son, O Zeus, exacting a full penalty.

Alas, O house! the fiend begins her dance of death without the cymbal's crash, with no glad waving of the wine-god's staff.

Woe to these halls toward bloodshed she moves, and not to pour libations of the juice of the grape.

O children, haste to fly; that is the chant of death her piping plays.

Ah, yes! he is chasing the children. Never, ah! never will Madness lead her revel rout in vain.

Ah misery!
Ah me! how I lament that aged sire, that mother too that bore his babes in vain.

Look! look!
A tempest rocks the house; the roof is falling with it.
Oh! what art thou doing, son of Zeus?
Thou art sending hell's confusion against thy house, as erst did Pallas on Enceladus.

[A MESSENGER enters from the palace.]

MESSENGER
Ye hoary men of eld!

CHORUS
Why, oh! why this loud address to me?

MESSENGER
Awful is the sight within!

CHORUS

No need for me to call another to announce that.

MESSENGER

Dead lie the children.

CHORUS

Alas!

MESSENGER

Ah weep! for here is cause for weeping.

CHORUS

A cruel murder, wrought by parents' hands!

MESSENGER

No words can utter more than we have suffered.

CHORUS

What, canst thou prove this piteous ruin was a father's outrage on his children? Tell me how these heaven-sent woes came rushing on the house; say how the children met their sad mischance.

MESSENGER

Victims to purify the house were stationed before the altar of Zeus, for Heracles had slain and cast from his halls the king of the land. There stood his group of lovely children, with his sire and Megara; and already the basket was being passed round the altar, and we were keeping holy silence. But just as Alcmena's son was bringing the torch in his right hand to dip it in the holy water, he stopped without a word. And as their father lingered, his children looked at him; and lo! he was changed; his eyes were rolling; he was distraught; his eyeballs were bloodshot and starting from their sockets, and foam was oozing down his bearded cheek. Anon he spoke, laughing the while a madman's laugh, "Father, why should I sacrifice before I have slain Eurystheus, why kindle the purifying flame and have the toil twice over, when I might at one stroke so fairly end it all? Soon as I have brought the head of Eurystheus hither, I will cleanse my hands for those already slain. Spill the water, cast the baskets from your hands. Ho! give me now my bow and club! To famed Mycenae will I go; crow-bars and pick-axes must I take, for I will heave from their very base with iron levers those city-walls which the Cyclopes squared with red plumb-line and mason's tools."

Then he set out, and though he had no chariot there, he thought he had, and was for mounting to its seat, and using a goad as though his fingers really held one. A twofold feeling filled his servants' breasts, half amusement, and half fear; and one looking to his neighbour said, "Is our master making sport for us, or is he mad?" But he the while was pacing to and fro in his house; and, rushing into the men's chamber, he thought he had reached the city of Nisus, albeit he had gone into his own halls. So he threw himself upon the floor, as if he were there, and made ready to feast. But after waiting a brief space he began saying he was on his way to the plains amid the valleys of the Isthmus; and then stripping himself of his mantle, he fell to competing with an imaginary rival, o'er whom he proclaimed himself victor with his own voice, calling on imaginary spectators to listen. Next, fancy carrying him to Mycenae, he was uttering fearful threats against Eurystheus. Meantime his father caught him by his stalwart arm, and thus addressed him, "My son, what meanest thou hereby? What strange doings are these? Can it be that the blood of thy late victims has driven thee frantic?" But he, supposing it was the father of Eurystheus striving in abject supplication to touch his hand, thrust him aside, and then against his own children aimed his bow and made ready his quiver, thinking to slay the sons of Eurystheus. And they in wild affright darted hither and thither, one to his hapless mother's skirts, another to the shadow of a pillar, while a third cowered 'neath the altar like a bird. Then cried their mother, "O father, what art thou doing? dost mean to slay thy children?" Likewise his aged sire and all the gathered servants cried aloud. But he, hunting the child round and round, the column, in dreadful circles, and coming face to face with him shot him to the heart; and he fell upon his back, sprinkling the stone pillars with blood as he gasped out his life. Then did Heracles shout for joy and boasted loud, "Here lies one of Eurystheus' brood dead at my feet, atoning for his father's hate." Against a second did he aim his bow, who had crouched at the altar's foot thinking to escape unseen. But ere he fired, the poor child threw himself at his father's knees, and, flinging his hand to reach his beard or neck, cried, "Oh! slay me not, dear father mine! I am thy child, thine own; 'tis no son of Eurystheus thou wilt slay."

But that other, with savage Gorgon-scowl, as the child now stood in range of his baleful archery, smote him on the head, as smites a smith his molten iron, bringing down his club upon the fair-haired boy, and crushed the bones. The second caught, away he hies to add a third victim to the other twain. But ere he could, the poor mother caught up her babe and carried him within the house and shut the doors; forthwith the madman, as though he really were at the Cyclopean walls, prizes open the doors with levers, and, hurling down their posts, with one fell shaft laid low his wife and child. Then in wild career he starts to slay his aged sire; but lo! there came a phantom,-so it seemed to us on-lookers,-Of Pallas, with plumed helm, brandishing a spear; and she hurled a rock against the breast of Heracles, which stayed him from his frenzied thirst for blood and plunged him into sleep; to the ground he fell, smiting his back against a column that had fallen on the floor in twain when the roof fell in. Thereon we rallied from our flight, and with the old man's aid bound him fast with knotted cords to the pillar, that on his awakening he might do no further evil. So there he sleeps, poor wretch! a sleep that is not blest, having murdered wife and children; nay, for my part know not any son of man more miserable than he.

[The **MESSENGER** withdraws.]

CHORUS [singing]
That murder wrought by the daughters of Danaus, whereof my native Argos wots, was formerly the most famous and notorious in Hellas; but this hath surpassed and outdone those previous horrors. I could tell of the murder of that poor son of Zeus, whom Procne, mother of an only child, slew and offered to the Muses; but thou hadst three children, wretched parent, and all of them hast thou in thy frenzy slain. What groans or wails, what funeral dirge, or chant of death am I to raise? Alas and woe! see, the bolted doors of the lofty palace are being rolled apart. Ah me! behold these children lying dead before their wretched father, who is sunk in awful slumber after shedding their blood. Round him are bonds and cords, made fast with many a knot about the body of Heracles, and lashed to the stone columns of his house. While he, the aged sire, like mother-bird wailing her unfledged brood, comes hasting hither with halting steps on his bitter journey.

[The central doors of the palace have opened and have disclosed **HERACLES** lying asleep, bound to a shattered column. **AMPHITRYON** steps out. The following lines between **AMPHITRYON** and the **CHORUS** are chanted responsively.]

AMPHITRYON
Softly, softly! ye aged sons of Thebes, let him sleep on and forget his sorrows.

CHORUS

For thee, old friend, I weep and mourn, for the children too and that victorious chief.

AMPHITRYON

Stand further off, make no noise nor outcry, rouse him not from his calm deep slumber.

CHORUS

O horrible! all this blood-

AMPHITRYON

Hush, hush! ye will be my ruin.

CHORUS

That he has spilt is rising up against him.

AMPHITRYON

Gently raise your dirge of woe, old friends; lest he wake, and, bursting his bonds, destroy the city, rend his sire, and dash his house to pieces.

CHORUS

I cannot, cannot-

AMPHITRYON

Hush! let me note his breathing; come, let me put my ear close.

CHORUS

Is he sleeping?

AMPHITRYON

Aye, that is he, a deathly sleep, having slain wife and children with the arrows of his twanging bow.

CHORUS

Ah! mourn—

AMPHITRYON

I do.

CHORUS

The children's death;

AMPHITRYON

Ah me!

CHORUS

And thy own son's doom.

AMPHITRYON

Ah misery!

CHORUS
Old friend—

AMPHITRYON
Hush! hush! he is turning, he is waking! Oh Oh! let me hide myself beneath the covert of yon roof.

CHORUS
Courage! darkness still broods o'er thy son's eye.

AMPHITRYON
Oh! beware; 'tis not that I shrink from leaving the light after my miseries, poor wretch! but should he slay me that am his father, then will he be devising woe on woe, and to the avenging curse will add a parent's blood.

CHORUS
Well for thee hadst thou died in that day, when, to win thy wife, thou didst go forth to exact vengeance for her slain brethren by sacking the Taphians' sea-beat town.

AMPHITRYON
Fly, fly, my aged friends, haste from before the palace, escape his waking fury! For soon will he heap up fresh carnage on the old, ranging wildly once more through the streets of Thebes.

CHORUS
O Zeus, why hast thou shown such savage hate against thine own son and plunged him in this sea of troubles?

HERACLES [waking]
Aha! my breath returns; I am alive; and my eyes see, opening on the sky and earth and yon sun's darting beam; but how my senses reel! in what strange turmoil am I plunged! my fevered breath in quick spasmodic gasps escapes my lungs. How now? why am I lying here, made fast with cables like a ship, my brawny chest and arms tied to a shattered piece of masonry, with corpses for my neighbours; while o'er the floor my bow and arrows are scattered, that erst like trusty squires to my arm both kept me safe and were kept safe of me? Surely I am not come a second time to Hades' halls, having just returned from thence for Eurystheus? No, I do not see Sisyphus with his stone, or Pluto, or his queen, Demeter's child. Surely I am distraught; I cannot remember where I am. Ho, there! which of my friends is near or far to help me in my ignorance? For I have no clear knowledge of things once familiar.

AMPHITRYON
My aged friends, shall I approach the scene of my sorrow?

LEADER OF THE CHORUS
Yes, and let me go with thee, nor desert thee in thy trouble.

HERACLES
Father, why dost thou weep and veil thy eyes, standing aloof from thy beloved son?

AMPHITRYON
My child! mine still, for all thy misery.

HERACLES
Why, what is there so sad in my case that thou dost weep?

AMPHITRYON
That which might make any of the gods weep, were he to suffer so.

HERACLES
A bold assertion that, but thou art not yet explaining what has happened.

AMPHITRYON
Thine own eyes see that, if by this time thou are restored to thy senses.

HERACLES
Fill in thy sketch if any change awaits my life.

AMPHITRYON
I will explain, if thou art no longer mad as a fiend of hell.

HERACLES
God help us! what suspicions these dark hints of thine again excite!

AMPHITRYON
I am still doubtful whether thou art in thy sober senses.

HERACLES
I never remember being mad.

AMPHITRYON
Am I to loose my son, old friends, or what?

HERACLES
Loose and say who bound me; for I feel shame at this.

AMPHITRYON
Rest content with what thou knowest of thy woes; the rest forego.

HERACLES
Enough! I have no wish to probe thy silence.

AMPHITRYON
O Zeus, dost thou behold these deeds proceeding from the throne of Hera?

HERACLES
What! have I suffered something from her enmity?

AMPHITRYON

A truce to the goddess! attend to thy own troubles.

HERACLES

I am undone; what mischance wilt thou unfold?

AMPHITRYON

See here the corpses of thy children.

HERACLES

O horror! what hideous sight is here? ah me!

AMPHITRYON

My son, against thy children hast thou waged unnatural war.

HERACLES

War! what meanst thou? who killed these?

AMPHITRYON

Thou and thy bow and some god, whoso he be that is to blame.

HERACLES

What sayst thou? what have I done? Speak, father, thou messenger of evil.

AMPHITRYON

Thou wert distraught; 'tis a sad explanation thou art asking.

HERACLES

Was it I that slew my wife also?

AMPHITRYON

Thy own unaided arm hath done all this.

HERACLES

Ah, woe is me! a cloud of sorrow wraps me round.

AMPHITRYON

The reason this that I lament thy fate.

HERACLES

Did I dash my house to pieces or incite others thereto?

AMPHITRYON

Naught know I save this, that thou art utterly undone.

HERACLES

Where did my frenzy seize me? where did it destroy me?

AMPHITRYON

In the moment thou wert purifying thyself with fire at the altar.

HERACLES

Ah me! why do I spare my own life when I have taken that of my dear children? Shall I not hasten to leap from some sheer rock, or aim the sword against my heart and avenge my children's blood, or burn my body in the fire and so avert from my life the infamy which now awaits me?

But hither I see Theseus coming to check my deadly counsels, my kinsman and friend. Now shall I stand revealed, and the dearest of my friends will see the pollution I have incurred by my children's murder. Ah, woe is me! what am I to do? Where can I find release from my sorrows? shall I take wings or plunge beneath the earth? Come, let me veil my head in darkness; for I am ashamed of the evil I have done, and, since for these I have incurred fresh blood-guiltiness, I would fain not harm the innocent.

[**THESEUS** and his **RETINUE** enter.]

THESEUS

I am come, and others with me, young warriors from the land of Athens, encamped by the streams of Asopus, to help thy son, old friend. For a rumour reached the city of the Erechtheidae, that Lycus had usurped the sceptre of this land and was become your enemy even to battle. Wherefore I came making recompense for the former kindness of Heracles in saving me from the world below, if haply ye have any need of such aid as I or my allies can give, old prince.

Ha! what means this heap of dead upon the floor? Surely I have not delayed too long and come too late to check new ills? Who slew these children? whose wife is this I see? Boys do not go to battle; nay, it must be some other strange mischance I here discover.

[The following lines between **THESEUS** and **AMPHITRYON** are chanted responsively.]

AMPHITRYON

O king, whose home is that olive-clad hill!

THESEUS

Why this piteous prelude in addressing me?

AMPHITRYON

Heaven has afflicted us with grievous suffering.

THESEUS

Whose be these children, o'er whom thou weepest?

AMPHITRYON

My own son's children, woe to him! their father and butcher both was he, hardening his heart to the bloody deed.

THESEUS

Hush good words only!

AMPHITRYON
I would I could obey!

THESEUS
What dreadful words!

AMPHITRYON
Fortune has spread her wings, and we are ruined, ruined.

THESEUS
What meanest thou? what hath he done?

AMPHITRYON
Slain them in a wild fit of frenzy with arrows dipped in the venom of the hundred-headed hydra.

THESEUS
This is Hera's work; but who lies there among the dead, old man?

AMPHITRYON
My son, my own enduring son, that marched with gods to Phlegra's plain, there to battle with giants and slay them, warrior that he was.

THESEUS
Ah, woe for him! whose fortune was e'er so curst as his?

AMPHITRYON
Never wilt thou find another that hath borne a larger share of suffering or been more fatally deceived.

THESEUS
Why doth he veil his head, poor wretch, in his robe?

AMPHITRYON
He is ashamed to meet thine eye; his kinsman's kind intent
and his children's blood make him abashed.

THESEUS
But I come to sympathize; uncover him.

AMPHITRYON
My son, remove that mantle from thine eyes, throw it from thee, show thy fare unto the sun; a counterpoise to weeping is battling for the mastery. In suppliant wise I entreat thee, as I grasp thy beard, thy knees, thy hands, and let fall the tear from my old eyes. O my child! restrain thy savage lion-like temper, for thou art rushing forth on an unholy course of bloodshed, eager to join woe to woe.

THESEUS
Ho! To thee I call who art huddled there in thy misery, show to they friends thy face; for no darkness is black enough to hide thy sad mischance. Why dost thou wave thy hand at me, signifying murder? is it that I may not be polluted by speaking with thee? If I share thy misfortune, what is that to me? For if I

too had luck in days gone by, must refer it to the time when thou didst bring me safe from the dead to the light of life. I hate a friend whose gratitude grows old; one who ready to enjoy his friends' prosperity but unwilling to sail in the same ship with them when their fortune lours. Arise, unveil thy head, poor wretch! and look on me. The gallant soul endures without a word such blows as heaven deals.

HERACLES
O Theseus, didst thou witness this struggle with my children?

THESEUS
I heard of it, and now I see the horrors thou meanest.

HERACLES
Why then hast thou unveiled my head to the sun?

THESEUS
Why have I? Thou, a man, canst not pollute what is of God.

HERACLES
Fly, luckless wretch, from my unholy taint.

THESEUS
The avenging fiend goes not forth from friend to friend.

HERACLES
For this I thank thee; I do not regret the service I did thee.

THESEUS
While I, for kindness then received, now show my pity for thee.

HERACLES
Ah yes! I am piteous, a murderer of my sons.

THESEUS
I weep for thee in thy changed fortunes.

HERACLES
Didst ever find another more afflicted?

THESEUS
Thy misfortunes reach from earth to heaven.

HERACLES
Therefore am I resolved on death.

THESEUS
Dost thou suppose the gods attend to these thy threats?

HERACLES

Remorseless hath heaven been to me; so I will prove the like to it.

THESEUS
Hush! lest thy presumption add to thy sufferings.

HERACLES
My barque is freighted full with sorrow; there is no room to stow aught further.

THESEUS
What wilt thou do? whither is thy fury drifting thee?

HERACLES
I will die and return to that world below whence I have just come.

THESEUS
Such language is fit for any common fellow.

HERACLES
Ah! thine is the advice of one outside sorrow's pale.

THESEUS
Are these indeed the words of Heracles, the much-enduring?

HERACLES
Though never so much as this. Endurance must have a limit.

THESEUS
Is this man's benefactor, his chiefest friend?

HERACLES
Man brings no help to me; no! Hera has her way.

THESEUS
Never will Hellas suffer thee to die through sheer perversity.

HERACLES
Hear me a moment, that I may enter the lists with words in answer to thy admonitions; and I will unfold to thee why life now as well as formerly has been unbearable to me. First I am the son of a man who incurred the guilt of blood, before he married my mother Alcmena, by slaying her aged sire. Now when the foundation is badly laid at birth, needs must the race be cursed with woe; and Zeus, whoever this Zeus may be, begot me as a butt for Hera's hate; yet be not thou vexed thereat, old man; for thee rather than Zeus do I regard as my father. Then whilst I was yet being suckled, that bride of Zeus did foist into my cradle fearsome snakes to compass my death. After I was grown to man's estate, of all the toils I then endured what need to tell? of all the lions, Typhons triple-bodied, and giants that I slew; or of the battle I won against the hosts of four-legged Centaurs? or how when I had killed the hydra, that monster with a ring of heads with power to grow again, I passed through countless other toils besides and came unto the dead to fetch to the light at the bidding of Eurystheus the three-headed hound, hell's porter. Last, ah, woe is me have I perpetrated this bloody deed to crown the sorrows of my house with my

children's murder. To this sore strait am I come; no longer may I dwell in Thebes, the city that I love; for suppose I stay, to what temple or gathering of friends shall I repair? For mine is no curse that invites address. Shall I to Argos? how can I, when I am an exile from my country? Well, is there a single other city I can fly to? And if there were, am I to be looked at askance as a marked man, branded by cruel stabbing tongues, "Is not this the son of Zeus that once murdered wife and children? Plague take him from the land!"

Now to one who was erst called happy, such changes are a grievous thing; though he who is always unfortunate feels no such pain, for sorrow is his birthright. This, methinks, is the piteous pass I shall one day come to; for earth will cry out forbidding me to touch her, the sea and the river-springs will refuse me a crossing, and I shall become like Ixion who revolves in chains upon that wheel. Wherefore this is best, that henceforth I be seen by none of the Hellenes, amongst whom in happier days I lived in bliss. What right have I to live? what profit can I have in the possession of a useless, impious life? So let that noble wife of Zeus break forth in dancing, beating with buskined foot on heaven's bright floor; for now hath she worked her heart's desire in utterly confounding the chiefest of Hellas' sons. Who would pray to such a goddess? Her jealousy of Zeus for his love of a woman hath destroyed the benefactors of Hellas, guiltless though they were.

LEADER OF THE CHORUS
This is the work of none other of the gods than the wife of Zeus; thou art right in that surmise.

THESEUS
I cannot counsel you to die rather than to go on suffering. There is not a man alive that hath wholly 'scaped misfortune's taint, nor any god either, if what poets sing is true. Have they not intermarried in ways that law forbids? Have they not thrown fathers into ignominious chains to gain the sovereign power? Still they inhabit Olympus and brave the issue of their crimes. And yet what shalt thou say in thy defence, if thou, child of man, dost kick against the pricks of fate, while they do not? Nay, then, leave Thebes in compliance with the law, and come with me to the city of Pallas. There, when I have purified thee of thy pollution, will I give thee temples and the half of all I have. Yea, I will give thee all those presents I received from the citizens for saving their children, seven sons and daughters seven, on the day I slew the bull of Crete; for I have plots of land assigned me throughout the country; these shall henceforth be called after thee by men, whilst thou livest; and at thy death, when thou art gone to Hades' halls, the city of Athens shall unite in exalting thy honour with sacrifices and a monument of stone. For 'tis a noble crown for citizens to win from Hellas, even a reputation fair, by helping a man of worth. This is the return that I will make thee for saving me, for now art thou in need of friends. But when heaven delights to honour a man, he has no need of friends; for the god's aid, when he chooses to give it, is enough.

HERACLES
Alas! this is quite beside the question of my troubles. For my part, I do not believe that the gods indulge in unholy unions; and as for putting fetters on parents' hands, I have never thought that worthy of belief, nor will I now be so persuaded, nor again that one god is naturally lord and master of another. For the deity, if he be really such, has no wants; these are miserable fictions of the poets. But I, for all my piteous plight, reflected whether I should let myself be branded as a coward for giving up my life. For whoso schooleth not his frail mortal nature to bear fate's buffets as he ought, will never be able to withstand even a man's weapon. I will harden my heart against death and seek thy city, with grateful thanks for all thou offerest me.

[He weeps.]

Of countless troubles have I tasted, God knows, but never yet did faint at any or shed a single tear; nay, nor ever dreamt that I should come to this, to let the tear-drop fall. But now, it seems, I must be fortune's slave. Well, let it pass; old father mine, thou seest me go forth to exile, and in me beholdest my own children's murderer. Give them burial and lay them out in death with the tribute of a tear, for the law forbids my doing so. Rest their heads upon their mother's bosom and fold them in her arms, sad pledges of our union, whom I, alas! unwittingly did slay. And when thou hast buried these dead, live on here still, in bitterness maybe, but still constrain thy soul to share my sorrows. O children! he who begat you, your own father, hath been your destroyer, and ye have had no profit of my triumphs, all my restless toil to win you a fair name in life, a glorious guerdon from a sire. Thee too, unhappy wife, this hand hath slain, a poor return to make thee for preserving mine honour so safe, for all the weary watch thou long hast kept within my house. Alas for you, my wife, my sons! and woe for me, how sad my lot, cut off from wife and child! Ah! these kisses, bitter-sweet! these weapons which 'tis pain to own! I am not sure whether to keep or let them go; dangling at my side they thus will say, "With us didst thou destroy children and wife; we are thy children's slayers, and thou keepest us." Shall I carry them after that? what answer can I make? Yet, am I to strip me of these weapons, the comrades of my glorious career in Hellas, and put myself thereby in the power of my foes, to die a death of shame? No! I must not let them go, but keep them, though it grieve me. In one thing, Theseus, help my misery; come to Argos with me and aid in settling my reward for bringing Cerberus thither; lest, if I go all alone, my sorrow for my sons do me some hurt.

O land of Cadmus, and all ye folk of Thebes! cut off your hair, and mourn with me; go to my children's burial, and with united dirge lament alike the dead and me; for on all of us hath Hera inflicted the same cruel blow of destruction.

THESEUS
Rise, unhappy man! thou hast had thy fill of tears.

HERACLES
I cannot rise; my limbs are rooted here.

THESEUS
Yea, even the strong are o'erthrown by misfortunes.

HERACLES
Ah! would I could grow into a stone upon this spot, oblivious of trouble!

THESEUS
Peace! give thy hand to a friend and helper.

HERACLES
Nay, let me not wipe off the blood upon thy robe.

THESEUS
Wipe it off and spare not; I will not say thee nay.

HERACLES

Reft of my own sons, I find thee as a son to me.

THESEUS
Throw thy arm about my neck; I will be thy guide.

HERACLES
A pair of friends in sooth are we, but one a man of sorrows. Ah! aged sire, this is the kind of man to make a friend.

AMPHITRYON
Blest in her sons, the country that gave him birth!

HERACLES
O Theseus, turn me back again to see my babes.

THESEUS
What charm dost think to find in this to soothe thy soul?

HERACLES
I long to do so, and would fain embrace my sire.

AMPHITRYON
Here am I, my son; thy wish is no less dear to me.

THESEUS
Hast thou so short a memory for thy troubles?

HERACLES
All that I endured of yore was easier to bear than this.

THESEUS
If men see thee play the woman, they will scoff.

HERACLES
Have I by living grown so abject in thy sight? 'twas not so once, methinks.

THESEUS
Aye, too much so; for how dost show thyself the glorious Heracles of yore?

HERACLES
What about thyself? what kind of hero wert thou when in trouble in the world below?

THESEUS
I was worse than anyone as far as courage went.

HERACLES
How then canst thou say of me, that I am abased by my troubles?

THESEUS
Forward!

HERACLES
Farewell, my aged sire!

AMPHITRYON
Farewell to thee, my son!

HERACLES
Bury my children as I said.

AMPHITRYON
But who will bury me, my son?

HERACLES
I will.

AMPHITRYON
When wilt thou come?

HERACLES
After thou hast buried my children.

AMPHITRYON
How?

HERACLES
I will fetch thee from Thebes to Athens. But carry my children within, a grievous burden to the earth. And I, after ruining my house by deeds of shame, will follow in the wake of Theseus, totally destroyed. Whoso prefers wealth or might to the possession of good friends, thinketh amiss.

[**THESEUS** and his attendants lead **HERACLES** away.]

CHORUS [chanting]
With grief and many a bitter tear we go our way, robbed of all we prized most dearly.

Euripides – A Short Biography

Euripides is rightly lauded as one of the great dramatists of all time. In his lifetime, he wrote over 90 plays and although only 18 have survived they reveal the scope and reach of his genius.

Euripides is identified with many theatrical innovations that have influenced drama all the way down to modern times, especially in the representation of traditional, mythical heroes as ordinary people in extraordinary circumstances. This new approach led him to pioneer developments that later writers would adapt to comedy. Yet he also became "the most tragic of poets", focusing on the inner lives and motives of his characters in a way previously unknown. He was "the creator of...that cage which is the theatre of Shakespeare's Othello, Racine's Phèdre, of Ibsen and Strindberg," in which "...imprisoned men and women destroy each other by the intensity of their loves and hates", and yet he was also the literary ancestor of comic dramatists as diverse as Menander and George Bernard Shaw.

As would be expected from a life lived 2,500 years ago, details of it are few and far between. Accounts of his life, written down the ages, do exist but whether much is reliable or surmised is open to debate.

Most accounts agree that he was born on Salamis Island around 480 BC, to mother Cleito and father Mnesarchus, a retailer who lived in a village near Athens. Upon the receipt of an oracle saying that his son was fated to win "crowns of victory", Mnesarchus insisted that the boy should train for a career in athletics.

His education was not only confined to athletics: he also studied painting and philosophy under the masters Prodicus and Anaxagoras.

However, what became quickly very clear was that athletics was not to be his way to win crowns of victory. Euripides had been lucky enough to have been born in the era as the other two masters of Greek Tragedy; Sophocles and Æschylus. It was in their footsteps that he was destined to follow.

His first play was performed some thirteen years after the first of Socrates plays and a mere three years after Æschylus had written his classic The Oristria.

Theatre was becoming a very important part of the Greek culture. The Dionysia, held annually, was the most important festival of theatre and second only to the fore-runner of the Olympic games, the Panathenia, held every four years, in its appeal. It was a large festival in ancient Athens in honor of the god Dionysus, the central events of which were the theatrical performances of dramatic tragedies and, from 487 BC, comedies. The Dionysia actually consisted of two related festivals, the Rural Dionysia and the City Dionysia, which took place in different parts of the year.

Euripides first competed in the City Dionysia, in 455 BC, one year after the death of Æschylus, and, incredibly, it was not until 441 BC that he won first prize. His final competition in Athens was in 408 BC. However, The Bacchae and Iphigenia in Aulis were performed after his death in 405 BC and first prize was awarded posthumously. Altogether his plays won first prize only five times.

His plays, and those of Æschylus and Sophocles, indicate a difference in outlook between the three men, most easily explained as a generational gap, although with three great talents overlapping the driving forces may have pushed individual styles onwards perhaps faster than they may otherwise have done. Æschylus still looked back to the archaic period, Sophocles was in transition between periods, and Euripides was fully bonded with the new spirit of the classical age. When Euripides' plays are sequenced in time, they also show a developing pattern:

An early period of high tragedy (Medea, Hippolytus)
A patriotic period at the outset of the Peloponnesian War (Children of Hercules, Suppliants)
A middle period of disillusionment at the senselessness of war (Hecuba, Women of Troy)
An escapist period with a focus on romantic intrigue (Ion, Iphigenia in Tauris, Helen)
A final period of tragic despair (Orestes, Phoenician Women, Bacchae)

However, with over three quarters of his plays lost it is difficult to be certain as to whether the other works would also represent this development (e.g., Iphigenia at Aulis is dated with the 'despairing' Bacchae, yet it contains elements that became typical of New Comedy). In the Bacchae, he restores the chorus and messenger speech to their traditional role in the tragic plot, and the play appears to be the culmination of a regressive or archaizing tendency in his later works.

In one of his earliest surviving plays, Medea, includes a speech that he seems to have written in defence of himself as an intellectual ahead of his time, and to further challenge the times he has put the words in the mouth of the play's heroine:

"If you introduce new, intelligent ideas to fools, you will be thought frivolous, not intelligent. On the other hand, if you do get a reputation for surpassing those who are supposed to be intellectually sophisticated, you will seem to be a thorn in the city's flesh. This is what has happened to me."— Medea.

As we know Athenian tragedies during Euripides' lifetime were a public contest between playwrights. The state funded that contest and awarded prizes to the winners. The language was spoken and sung verse, the performance area included a circular floor or orchestra where the chorus could dance, a space for actors (usually three speaking actors in Euripides' time), a backdrop or skene and some special effects: an ekkyklema (used to bring the skene's "indoors" outdoors) and a mechane (used to lift actors in the air, as in deus ex machina). With the introduction of the third actor (an innovation attributed to Sophocles), acting also began to be regarded as a skill to be rewarded with prizes, requiring a long apprenticeship in the chorus. Euripides and other playwrights accordingly composed more and more arias for accomplished actors to sing and this tendency becomes more marked in his later plays: tragedy for him was a living and ever-changing genre.

Accounts by the famed comic poet, Aristophanes, characterise Euripides as a spokesman for destructive, new ideas, that mirror or help to bring about declining standards in both society and tragedy. However, 5th century tragedy was a social gathering for "carrying out quite publicly the maintenance and development of mental infrastructure" and it offered spectators a "platform for an utterly unique form of institutionalized discussion". A dramatist's role was not just to entertain but also to educate his fellow citizens—he was expected to have a message. Clearly this use of drama to democratize discussion was a very useful tool for all sides. Traditional myth provided the subject matter but the dramatist was meant to be innovative so as to sustain interest, which led to novel characterization of heroic figures and to use the mythical past to talk about present issues. The difference between Euripides and his older colleagues was, again, one of degree: his characters talked about the present more controversially and more pointedly than did those of Æschylus and Sophocles, sometimes even challenging the democratic order. Thus, for example, Odysseus is represented in Hecuba as "agile-minded, sweet-talking, demos-pleasing" i.e., a type of the war-time demagogues that were active in Athens during the Peloponnesian War. His concept is pleasingly simple. He retains the old stories and myths as well as the great names of the past and places them in the lives of contemporary Athenians thereby immediately help the audience understand it from the point of view of their own lives.

As mouthpieces for contemporary issues, they all seem to have had at least an elementary course in public speaking. Sometimes the dialogue often contrasts so strongly with the mythical and heroic setting, it looks as if Euripides aimed at parody, as for example in The Trojan Women, where the heroine's rationalized prayer provokes comment from Menelaus:

Hecuba:...O Zeus, whether you are the Law of Necessity in nature, or the Law of Reason in man, hear my prayers. You are everywhere, pursuing your noiseless path, ordering the affairs of mortals according to justice.

Menelaus: What's this? You are starting a new fashion in prayer.

Athenian citizens were familiar with rhetoric in the assembly and law courts, and some scholars believe that Euripides was more interested in his characters as speakers with cases to argue than as characters with lifelike personalities. They are self-conscious about speaking formally and their rhetoric is shown to be flawed, as if Euripides was exploring the problematical nature of language and communication: "For speech points in three different directions at once, to the speaker, to the person addressed, to the features in the world it describes, and each of these directions can be felt as skewed". Thus in the example above, Hecuba presents herself as a sophisticated intellectual describing a rationalised cosmos yet the speech is ill-matched to her audience, Menelaus (an unsophisticated listener), and soon it is found not to suit the cosmos either (her infant grandson is brutally murdered by the victorious Greeks).

Æschylus and Sophocles were innovative, but Euripides could move easily between tragic, comic, romantic and political effects, a versatility that appears in individual plays and also over the course of his career. Potential for comedy lay in his use of 'contemporary' characters, in his sophisticated tone, his relatively informal Greek, and his ingenious use of plots centered on motifs that later became standard, such as the 'recognition scene'. Other tragedians also used recognition scenes but they were heroic in emphasis, as in Æschylus's The Libation Bearers, which Euripides parodied with his mundane treatment of it in Electra (Euripides was unique among the tragedians in incorporating theatrical criticism in his plays). Traditional myth, with its exotic settings, heroic adventures and epic battles, offered potential for romantic melodrama as well as for political comments on a war theme, so that his plays are an extraordinary mix of elements. The Trojan Women for example is a powerfully disturbing play on the theme of war's horrors, apparently critical of Athenian imperialism (it was composed in the aftermath of the Melian massacre and during the preparations for the Sicilian Expedition) yet it features the comic exchange between Menelaus and Hecuba quoted above and the chorus considers Athens, the "blessed land of Theus", to be a desirable refuge—such complexity and ambiguity are typical both of his "patriotic" and "anti-war" plays.

Tragic poets in the 5th century competed against one another at the City Dionysia, each with a tetralogy consisting of three tragedies and a satyr-play. The few extant fragments of satyr-plays attributed to Æschylus and Sophocles indicate that these were a loosely structured, simple and jovial form of entertainment. However, in Cyclops (the only complete Euripides satyr-play that survives) the entertainment is structured more like a tragedy and introduced a note of critical irony typical of his other work. His genre-bending inventiveness is shown above all in Alcestis, a blend of tragic and satyric elements. This fourth play in his tetralogy for 438 BC (i.e., it occupied the position conventionally reserved for satyr-plays) is a "tragedy" that features Heracles as a satyric hero in conventional satyr-play scenes, involving an arrival, a banquet, a victory over an ogre (in this case, Death), a happy ending, a feast and a departure to new adventures.

Euripides was also a great lyric poet. In Medea, for example, he composed for his city, Athens, "the noblest of her songs of praise". His lyric skills however are not just confined to individual poems: "A play of Euripides is a musical whole....one song echoes motifs from the preceding song, while introducing new ones."

Much of his life and his whole career coincided with the struggle between Athens and Sparta for hegemony in Greece but he didn't live to see the final defeat of his city.

It is said that he died in Macedonia after being attacked by the Molossian hounds of King Archelaus and that his cenotaph near Piraeus was struck by lightning—signs of his unique powers, whether for good or ill. In an account by Plutarch, the complete failure of the Sicilian expedition led Athenians to trade renditions of Euripides' lyrics to their enemies in return for food and drink (Life of Nicias 29). Plutarch is the source also for the story that the victorious Spartan generals, having planned the demolition of Athens and the enslavement of its people, grew merciful after being entertained at a banquet by lyrics from Euripides' play Electra: "they felt that it would be a barbarous act to annihilate a city which produced such men" (Life of Lysander).

In The Frogs, composed after Euripides and Æschylus were both dead, Aristophanes imagines the god Dionysus venturing down to Hades in search of a good poet to bring back to Athens. After a debate between the two deceased bards, the god brings Æschylus back to life as more useful to Athens on account of his wisdom, rejecting Euripides as merely clever. Such comic 'evidence' suggests that Athenians admired Euripides even while they mistrusted his intellectualism, at least during the long war with Sparta.

Euripides had a famous library—one of the first to be privately collected. Although he lived most of his life in the midst of the cultured society of Athens, and was in some respects a leader in it, he grew bitter and despondent over the fierce rivalries and greedy ambitions which ran through the city. He loved the seclusion of his house at Salamis, where it was said that he composed his dramas in a cave.

Euripides fell out of favour with his fellow Athenian citizens and retired to the court of Archelaus, king of Macedon, who treated him with consideration and affection.

At his death, in around 406BC, he was mourned by the king, who, refusing the request of the Athenians that his remains be carried back to the Greek city, buried him with much splendor within his own dominions. His tomb was placed at the confluence of two streams, near Arethusa in Macedonia, and a cenotaph was built to his memory on the road from Athens towards the Piraeus.

Euripides – A Concise Bibliography

Alcestis (438 BC)
Medea (431 BC)
Heracleidae (c. 430 BC)
Hippolytus (428 BC)
Andromache (c. 425 BC)
Hecuba (c. 424 BC)
The Suppliants (c. 423 BC)
Electra (c. 420 BC)
Heracles (c. 416 BC)
The Trojan Women (c. 415 BC)
Iphigenia in Tauris (c. 414 BC)
Ion (c. 414 BC)

Helen (c. 412 BC)
Phoenician Women (c. 410 BC)
Orestes (c.408 BC)
Bacchae (405 BC)
Iphigenia at Aulis (405 BC)
Rhesus
Cyclops

Peliades (455 BC)
Telephus (438 BC with Alcestis)
Alcmaeon in Psophis (438 BC with Alcestis)
Cretan Women (438 with Alcestis)
Cretans (c. 435 BC)
Philoctetes (431 BC with Medea)
Dictys (431 BC with Medea)
Theristai (satyr play, 431 BC with Medea)
Stheneboea (before 429 BC)
Bellerophon (c. 430 BC)
Cresphontes (ca. 425 BC)
Erechtheus (422 BC)
Phaethon (c. 420 BC)
Wise Melanippe (c. 420 BC)
Alexandros (415 BC with Trojan Women)
Palamedes (415 BC with Trojan Women)
Sisyphus (satyr play, 415 BC with Trojan Women)
Captive Melanippe (c. 412 BC)
Andromeda (412 BC with Helen)
Antiope (c. 410 BC)
Archelaus (c. 410 BC)
Hypsipyle (c. 410 BC)
Alcmaeon in Corinth (c. 405 BC) Won first prize as part of a trilogy with The Bacchae and Iphigenia in Aulis.

Aegeus
Aeolus
Alcmene
Alope, or Cercyon
Antigone
Auge
Autolycus
Busiris
Cadmus

Chrysippus
Danae
Epeius
Eurystheus
Hippolytus Veiled
Ino
Ixion
Lamia
Licymnius
Meleager
Mysians
Oedipus
Oeneus
Oenomaus
Peirithous
Peleus
Phoenix
Phrixus
Pleisthenes
Polyidus
Protesilaus
Reapers
Rhadamanthys
Sciron
Scyrians
Syleus
Temenidae
Temenos
Tennes
Theseus
Thyestes

www.ingramcontent.com/pod-product-compliance
Lightning Source LLC
Chambersburg PA
CBHW060102050426
42448CB00011B/2587

9 781787 371651